# UNRAVELING

## POEMS

BRANDON LEAKE

Andrews McMeel
PUBLISHING®

# CONFUSED

What's worse
A man who knows his flaws but isn't willing to change them
Or a man who is blinded to his own inadequacies
The answer is, both
Or neither
Or pride
Maybe pride is the root of this disease
That rots a man from the inside out
I know that my rewards lie up in Heaven
But God, is it wrong I want my flowers while I can still smell 'em
I'm just saying this ambition you've planted in my soul
Is starting to take control
And I too often confuse your voice
With my desires

# SANDCASTLES

I love building things
Specifically, I love building Sandcastles
I don't know why, but I get a thrill out of
Creating something, leaving, and then coming back the next day
To see if the tide has washed it away
The intricate and delicate nature of its construction intrigues me
At times, I consider myself an architect
Intricately designing my residence
And preparation is the key
Determining a location to build your foundation is a priority
Understand that any old place will not do
But there must be compatibility
You must be able to see yourself in this place
And once this is done, it's time to lay down the blueprints
To assess what is present and see
What you would like to turn this situation into
Is this merely fatal attractions, short-term reaction
Or is this home long-lasting
Once determined, then we can begin drawing it out
Smooth edges with curves in all the right places,
Glossy windows that not only let you see what's inside
But peer back at you as well
An attic filled with knowledge and memories
A living room full of love
And a doormat that says, "Brandon, You Are Welcome Here"
After this blueprint is made
Then you can begin to assemble your foundation
The collection of materials is a must
Try to fit all the trust, acceptance, care, honesty, and love you can
Into your pail
You can make more than one trip if needed
Scratch that, more than one trip will be needed
So don't forget to scoop in a lot of patience too
Now that you have all the materials

Let's get building
Constructing this place will take time
Trying to rush will only result in mistakes that you will one day have to fix
Or someone else will have to fix
So we advise wisdom and forbearance be the liquid bonds
That hold your sand assembly together
After the construction of your base is complete, then comes the fun part
The decorative aspects of home building
Choosing colors that suit your guys' demeanor
HDTVs to vividly recall all your memories
But leaving plenty of space to grow into
This place is starting to feel like home
So now the curtains can come down
All defenses are gone
Just transparency
Honesty is always the best policy
Except when it isn't
Except when the thoughts that linger in your mind
Begin to dry up the walls of your home
Making them dry bone brittle
And now you leave this place in search of what you once had
To only find that you don't know what you had 'til you left it
Then you return back the next day
Only to see that the cool ocean water
That once helped create this inhabitance
Has now claimed back what it gave
But that's okay because I love building things
Specifically, I love building Sandcastles
I don't know why but . . .
Wait
This all feels familiar

# HEIGHTS

My name is Brandon Leake
I spend a majority of my time
Tattooing words across my wounds
Cause I hear they heal best that way
I'm insecure about a lot of things
But being black in America
Has taught me the best way to camouflage
Is by overcompensating
Create a large enough of a facade
That the rest of the world will develop
An Elephant Complex about you
They'll be so close to all your beautiful parts
They won't even be able to tell
The elephant had been dying
The whole time they had been looking at it
I find peace in my conversations with God
But too oftentimes, I put Him on hold
To dialogue with my fears
I swear to Him it won't happen again
Knowing it will
Thinking about it, that's probably where my
Perfectionism comes from
I've never quite felt enough
Being on a pedestal doesn't really suit me
Probably cause I'm horrified of heights
But honestly, it's not that I'm afraid of heights
I'm more afraid of what happens when gravity
Wants to reintroduce me to my former self
For from the dust we were made
And to the dust we shall return
I'm just not ready to look in the mirror yet
I know there's so much more to learn
And way more for me to grow

I guess my biggest fear is living with regrets
Knowing that in this finite existence, I only got one shot
And if being black in America will teach you anything
It's that one bad shot is all it takes
Bang

# LIVING

I wonder what happened to the old me
The one who used to write poetry just for the thrill
Of seeing pen and paper dance
To the tune of his imagination
Used to craft stories out of thin air
As if this moment had enough magic left in it
To whisper itself eternal
But now it all seems so serious
So scripted
So concerned with the opinions of the ones who will hear it
The ones who will read it
The ones who will deem it not bloody enough
Ask for more of your corpse on the page
No one likes the living artist
The one who sees value in something other than the ending of things
I'm not searching for a new beginning
I'm somewhere in the middle
Not quite hopelessly searching
Yet not quite woefully unearthing
All of these dead parts of me
This time I'm . . .
I'm staying clean
Allowing for whatever flows from this soul
To touch paper and not care about the response it gets
Yeah . . .
It's cathartic knowing that despite judgment, I'll be okay
That my pen still deserves a place in existence
Even if you don't enjoy what it writes . . .
Yeah . . .
I'm finally starting to see less harmony in taxonomy
I don't need to continue to preserve what's lost
I can be just fine
Living

# BOTTOMLESS

My vision's a little blurry
The world seems to be moving in circles
Man, I think I might have had one too many
But I mean, at the start of my night, I said I would take it slow
Slow motion, however, wasn't what I ever intended to be moving in
Wait, is that me or is everyone around me just moving faster
I think I'll just take another drink on the rocks
Egghh . . .
I like the burn of it
It's weird
They said drinking this would help numb the pain
But I feel more now than I ever have
I feel the pain I tried to bury
I feel the love I want to ignore
I feel the cool of this drink evaporate
Under the heat of its sting
I feel out of control
But that's alright, cause we just living for tonight
Drinks up in the air
Let's end the night like we don't care about tomorrow
Or five minutes from now
Or our friends, family, responsibilities
We hope that tonight won't end at the end of this cup
So we can avoid the troubles of today
And not worry about tomorrow
So let us drink
Let us drink our sorrows down with the numbing chill of icy disregard
But the burning aftertaste of regret
Knowing that tomorrow we must return to reality
Knowing that we must return to the unemployment line
Knowing they will term you overqualified yet never give you a chance
Knowing we must return home to the lover
Whose touch leaves you black and blue

And when you try to explain
Your tongue ties itself cause it's tired of the lies
Our lives are hell already, so what need do we have for an afterlife
And people's false hope of things will get better;
Just give it some time
Does nothing but remind me of the millions of other times
People have uttered those words to me
And how when I finally got courage to hope once more
I was dragged by my ankles, beaten unconscious
Told I was worthless
Left for dead, and then "recused" by the same hands
So tell me who is to blame when the abuser and my savior are the
same person
But now I have a new lifeguard who is never asleep on duty
He would never hurt me and takes an edge off my painful existence . . .
Most of the time
But hell, nothing is foolproof right
He and I have been spending a lot of time together
Oftentimes, I wake up not remembering the night before
But it couldn't have been that bad, right
And if it was, he was gracious enough
To not let me remember it
And I love him for that

# UNSURE

The funniest part of isolation
Is that you don't have to be alone to feel it
Or not feel it
Or not feel anything
I don't really know intimacy
She's the acquaintance I hype up like we're really friends
When I couldn't tell you anything more about her than her name
I know love, but loving someone don't make you close
Just means you have enough of a pulse
To endure this beating
This constant reminder that somehow you're still here
Even though you don't feel like it
Sometimes I mistake my own reflection as a shadow
But it's more grounded than I am
And people don't understand
They see me on stage and wonder how I complain
Not recognizing I'm the only one up here
Me, myself, and a reflection I don't recognize
People applaud these poems
Just further justifies what lies in my mind
The only worthy parts of yourself are the ones they can take
Are the ones they accept
My skeleton is doing its best to claw its way out of this flesh
To join all the rest of its kin in my wardrobe
To escape from this stage to finally be itself
Raw and unkempt
But that's what isolation does
Forces you in the closet
Makes that space feel more comfortable
The closer isolation draws near
The further everything else is
And it's just you, yourself, and a reflection you finally recognize
People misunderstand that most isolated people
Are in a love-hate relationship with it

They recognize it's killing them
But the comfort that kind of death brings is maddening
So yes, I want freedom from this cage
But I'm the one holding the key
Most
Unsure
Of everything

# DANIELLE

I poured all the best of me into you
But when your pine box
Nestled into that grave
Just like you did in my arms
My envy burned as hot as the hell I was in
I was losing touch with myself
I never felt a pain this deep

# SAFE HAVEN

When I'm with you
I want to be able to crumble
I don't want to always have to be strong
I need something to fall upon
When the craziness of life erupts
And ash fills the air
Darkening my blue sky
I need to come back to you
So I can remove this heavy mask
And rest in the comfort of your arms
So I may be seen
Not just aesthetically viewed
But so you can see my soul
When I'm too afraid to show anyone else
Cause I'm doing my best to fight off these demons
But their persistence is draining
So please be my safe haven

# DEADLY FIRST LOVE

I love basketball
I grew up playing my entire life
You could always catch me
With a ball in hand
Crossover, step back, fadeaway
Swish
I loved basketball
It was the only
Fair thing in life I've ever experienced
For every time I stepped on the court
The score is always zero to zero
I didn't have to play the hero
I just had to play the game
Cause in this game of life
I entered in down fourteen
You ask what does that mean
It means that my margin for error
Is as thin as the line I have to cross
To get killed in a traffic stop
Down fourteen with two fouls against me
Looks like walking into an interview
While they question my credentials
As if my resume is fraudulent
Looks like fitting the description eight times out of ten
Looks like approaching with hands up
Avoiding cuffs, but bullets I was fresh outta luck
And in all honesty to this point
I am the exception
Have had enough skill and coaching
To maneuver around the defense to get to the cup
Had enough hustle to dive on loose balls
And enough faith that at the end of the day
God would reward my efforts

But most are not so fortunate
Play the game without a head coach
Forced to learn the rules of the game on their own
Committed too many turnovers
Picked up a couple of fouls
Now down twenty-two with only two fouls
Before he gotta hit the bench
He reaches and gets a clean steal
The whistle blows
He argues the call
They deem this resistance
Knowing what's at stake
He walks away
They deem this noncompliance
He throws his arms in frustration
Shots fired
Technical foul removed him from the game
God, what a shame
Another black man slain

# STARTER'S BLOCK

While talking about
The most recent murder
Of a black body by police
A white guy says
"If he wasn't guilty, then
Why'd he run from the cops?"
I respond, "Life's a race
The only way for
A black man to survive
Is running away from a gun
At the starter's block."

# KALEIDOSCOPE

There was this girl
Her heart a kaleidoscope
Of fatal attractions
But despite all of this, one thing never faded
Her love for love
No matter what love did
She always found her way back to it
She loved the way love feels
She loved love so much
She let love pimp her out
Cause love don't love her
Love loves what she'll do for love
Love loves what love can make her do
Love makes her strut and trick
Her emotional sanity
Love marionettes her self-worth
Cause she's only valuable
If love says she is
As love leverages her love for love
Against all the things that make her, her
And love knows she loves love so much
She won't step back and smell love's apathy
Love doesn't concern itself with her
Love concerns itself with
The perpetuation of itself
Love stole its secrets from the American Dream
Claiming it can be whatever you want it to be
When love is and always has been
Exactly what love is
And this ain't love
This is self-deprecation in sheep's clothing
Finding self-worth in all the wrong places
Will lead her to a quick death

But the way she rots inside will feel slow
Will leave her hollow
Only to be filled with the affection she had for love
And as she withers away, love says . . .
I love what you've done with yourself

# STRANGE FAMILIARITY

I don't know what draws me to you
Maybe it's your infectious smile
Or the way your hair sways in the wind
Maybe it's the way you laugh at my corny jokes
Or maybe it's knowing
You'll never truly be mine
There's something so enticing
About the beauty you can't pluck from the tree
Or maybe it's our strange familiarity that draws me near
Yeah, I think that's it
Our souls' distant lovers across eternities just searching for each other
Knowing they will never be one as they once were

# VICE VERSA

The greatest thief of joy is comparison
The easiest road to supremacy is comparing sin

# BOXES

In life, we pass sticks
And wonder why we can't escape carcinogen's curse
Reverse
Our life burns into flames just waiting to exhale
Is this hell
The block is hot
But they heart is cold
What an interesting paradox
Their lungs wheeze
BLACK POWER is killing me
While melanin folk
Steady think inside the box
Leading them same folk to residing inside the box

# PHARISEES

I don't want to be a mirage
I don't want to have
This visual presence of faith
But inwardly can't relate
I don't want for people to scream my name
For them to shout praises of my excellence
When my creator looks at me and says
"You know not your savior"
I don't want to be just another superficial servant
I don't want to be just another pharisee

# JOURNEY

This sweater of possibility that kept us both warm
Is now quickly unraveling
I guess with all possibilities, there are always some loose threads
And life must have caught this one under its boot
For the further we walk, the more undone we become
I think this journey is pulling us apart
Soon there will be nothing left but a trail of memories
I guess that's why they call life a journey

# THE SECRET LIFE OF TEACHERS

Growing up, my momma told me
Nothing stops a bullet
Like an education
But what happens when bullets
Get on the bus with you
When they get dropped off at school
When they race through the hallways
Wanting to spread your knowledge
Across the classroom
When did schools change
From being windows of opportunity
To bulletproof
We talk about creating safe spaces at schools
In being a teacher
The only safe space I see
Is under the desks of my classroom
Campuses are poor replacements
For war zones
For there is always casualty
Always a death
Whether it be of flesh and bone
Or of hope that there is a place
Where raised arms aren't so fatal
So to my government
I ask what shall you do
Shall we stay in this maddening cycle
Where access to guns is more readily available
Than access to health care
Where in some states, minors
Who aren't even allowed to drive or vote
Can tote steel like a fashion statement
I'm just saying
Insanity is perpetually doing the same thing

Expecting a different result
And this stretch of school shootings
Has confirmed our diagnosis
Now to our schools
It is our duty to create a culture
Where ostracism isn't so common
Where fellowship isn't so rare
These campuses need to be places to grow
But how can one do that
When they're continually masked in a shadow of fear
Whether it be from teachers or peers
Let our bodies be better lovers than fighters
So today, I choose to walk out
And walk up
I choose to speak out
Against a broken system
That listens to the NRA's song on replay
To muddle the sounds of children
Who are slain on their watch
And speak up for the
Students whom I see on the fringe
To let them know they are not alone
We all are broken people
Trying to find a place
Where our splintered edges fit best
And every morning, I fall on my knees and pray to God
Ask Jesus to be with my students and me today
That we wouldn't hit the six o'clock news
That we wouldn't be the next livestream on Facebook
That my wife's goodbye to me this morning
Wasn't so permanent
So dear government
I promise to make my classroom

A place where all students find love
A place where acceptance is more readily available than bullying
A place where lead only scrapes across paper
The question is
What are you going to do

# DISBELIEF

You drive me crazy
I know that doesn't seem like the most flattering thing to say
But hear me out
See, you drive me crazy
Cause every day, I'm trying to find new ways
To show you just how much I love you
Not because you demand it but because you deserve that
I want every day with you and me to be a brand new experience
Because I believe our today should never be like yesterday
And I don't believe in tomorrows cause I want to live in this moment
Where you and I are clumsily stammering through life together
Until the moment where we fall heart over soul for one another
But then again, it might already be a bit too late for that
Because I have already envisioned my forever with you
So I guess I do believe in tomorrows
But only because I hope you'll be a part of it

# BLACK JESUS

Seeing a brown-skinned man
With pierced hands
Strung up tree ornament pretty
For the eyes of a nation's
Moral elite ain't nothing new to me
It's probably the blackest thing I ever seen
The story of Jesus the Nazarene
Could have been a viral video in 2016
Seeing an innocent man's blood spilled
Due to the sin of another
Insert the name of Jesus where you see
Philando Castile, Trayvon Martin
Seeing an innocent man cracked open
Like strange fruit
For the appetites of a hungry crowd
That's Jesus, and though they were no Son of Man
I think back to Emmett Till,
I think back to Nat Turner,
I think back to the birth of a nation
This crucifixion is the birth of a nation
Where crosses made from the splintered edges of
Destructively dogmatic decrees lacking semblance of all empathy
Intersect with eyes blind to all the truth and love that fell off his lips
But are miraculously opened to the sight of his death
Up here on this cross is where the light of the world came to die
At the hand of his own people
To resurrect as freedom

# ADRIFT

Can I tell you something?
It's because of you that I made it
I know we've only known each other for a little while
But I've known you since the day I came out of the womb
I could hear your heart beat in unison with mine
A rhythmic pattern that intertwined our destinies
For you and I were made for each other
Do you believe that?
Because I have known you since before I ever physically met you
You see, our souls floated across eternity together before they
landed in these fleshly beings
Just like clouds
How nice would it be to be a cloud
To float adrift in the vastness of the sky
Carelessly witnessing the days and nights pass by
There being no true destination
Just merely embracing the freedom of the moment
For in this moment, let you and I be like clouds
Floating across the night sky with a courtside seat to the stars
And just an arms distance from the moon
A romantic affair only dictated by the air
And if it dares try and separate us from one another
Let it be for only a moment's notice
Cause seconds up here without you by my side seem like hours
For the stars don't shine as bright without you here since you are
the brightest among them
But in this moment of liminality, I shall love the freedom of the day
And let's just say
I won't mind aimlessly floating if I'm floating your way

# I REMEMBER

I remember history class
I remember the Declaration of Independence
I remember "that all men are created equal"
I remember listening to those words
I remember the Emancipation Proclamation
I remember believing that this was the day my freedom was set in stone
I remember my mind accepting this as truth
I remember feeling whole in my skin
I remember
I remember November 13, 2006
I remember walking back to campus
I remember that black and white vehicle mounting the curb
I remember the way his billy club spoke before he did
I remember being accused of a crime I didn't commit
I remember being told I fit the description
I remember being confident . . . that my innocence would be proven true
I remember my innocence not getting a chance to speak
I remember being called boy
I remember being called nigga
I remember my humanity shattering in his presence
I remember the heat of his glare like a field day in 1787
My raw cotton voice taken for his hateful profit
I remember not feeling so equal no mo'
I remember my teacher's voice
I remember him saying "that all men are created equal"
I remember that all men are created equal
I remember that all black men were considered evil
I remember that all black men are considered evil
I remember that black folks ain't considered people
I remember walking back to school
I remember
I remember thinking about my history class
I remember that confidence turning to fear

I remember wondering about all the history never told
I remember thinking about my books smelling like bleach
I remember
I remember looking back as my self-esteem hung like strange fruit
I remember looking my friend in the eye to see he lost just as much
as I did
I remember telling my coach what happened
I remember being told I shouldn't be angry
I remember telling them I'm not angry, I'm pissed
I remember the storm brewing in the bottom of my stomach
And having nowhere to unleash it without becoming another
casualty of this ongoing genocide
I remember two weeks passing by
I remember being called into my mother's room
I remember seeing two white boys pleading guilty for the crime I
was accused of
I remember feeling like justice hadn't been served
I remember I was still trying to assemble the pieces of my broken
humanity
I remember that officer's face
I remember my rage

# PAIN

I don't know what I'm feeling
It's . . .
Almost like death
But . . .
This pain makes me too alive

# ARTIFICIAL

Love is always sweeter like this
It's so much better
Blemished and imperfect
Loose ends make for great
Grabbing points
When it's too pristine and smooth
You can tell it's artificial

# DEAR REBECCA . . .

This is a letter to Rebecca
Her starry night skin speckled freckle
Her depression only wanted to connect the dots
Of these constellations
She a goddess
Reverse alchemy turns gold into stainless steel
As she whips it across her domain
Ripping open the sky
To rain down her pain
Her scars celestial trails
Of those freckled remnants
Covered by a cloudy haze
Of long sleeves and isolation
So no one could ever wish
On her shooting stars
Not even herself
All the nights she would wish
For sunrise
This perpetual midnight
Grew tiresome
Her starlight will grow dimmer
As eons of pain's complexity
Passed by
And other empathy grew thin
Existing becomes exhausting
When you're perceived
As your own problem
Her flame burning out
Suffocated by the vacuum
Of space between her soul and everyone else's
It's easier to fall from your own sky
When there's nothing holding you up
Space is a place where gravity doesn't exist

Yet don't things still fall from its graces
Don't things still come tumbling down to the ground
Don't all things eventually come tumbling down
Six feet under our feet
So what does it matter the cause of you getting there
Whether at the sword of your enemy
Or at the leisure of your own hand
We all know strange fruit tastes best
When you become it
But there is no fruit here
Just space and opportunity to become whatever you want
And all she's ever wanted to become
Is the greatest disappearing act
This galaxy has ever seen
To depart from existence in a blaze of glory
She could never attain on this side of eternity
Supernova spectacular
Her name written in constellations across
Her speckled, freckled skin
Maybe indeed sunrise is coming
With a passion that drips crimson

# REVERSE

What would life be like in reverse . . .
To be birthed from the ground
In the womb of a pine box
To grow healthier and stronger
To only die and return to embrace
Of the woman whose birth you mourned for

# A LETTER TO MY YOUNGER SELF

Hey me
I got a few pieces of advice for you
Don't be stupid, stupid
Don't hand out pieces of your heart so easily
You'll never get them back in the same condition you gave them
Sometimes that's a good thing
Stop putting loose candy in your pockets
It's gross
Don't look to reinvent yourself when things go wrong
Sometimes the reinventing is journeying through the pain
Stop whooping yourself every time you look in the mirror
The world causes enough wounds for you to deal with
And Jesus elected to adopt them scars
Though he is no masochist
Stop trying to be funny
You're not very good at it
And besides, as a black man
America loves to have the last laugh
Don't give them the satisfaction
Don't be dismayed by what they say
They will condemn you for being different
And they will condemn you for being the same
Some will say you're too radical
Others claim you're too reserved
The truth is found between two extremes
So let that be the solid ground you stand on
Don't forget to love yourself
Mirrors aren't only made for examining flaws
What I tell you before? Stop that whole "candy in the pocket thing"
Take a lesson from Trayvon that sweets can be deadly
Don't look to the future
Just embrace the now
As the good book says

What will worrying about tomorrow do for you
Will it add another day to your life
Or slow the gray of your hair
Don't stress it
Trust me, I'm fine
You grew up to be pretty cool
Naw, you didn't end up doing half of what you wanted to do in high school
But that's okay
Like I said, there is reinvention in the pain
And there is plenty of that come
Some uncomfortable funerals you have to attend
I guess I'll warn you of this
Burying parts of yourself ain't easy
But
Death is a breeze compared to living
Your greatest fight isn't against the grave
Christ already got that covered
It's against those demons called memories
The ones that harken you back to all your inadequacies
To all your faults
But that's okay
The past has its place
Just remember it is under your feet, not ahead of you
So as I was saying
Don't sweat it
The future is coming so we will meet soon
But if there is one thing I could tell you
That I wish I would have known
It's that
You're beautiful

# MARRIED PEOPLE'S POEMS

I was thinking about why I haven't written a love poem since I got married
And to be honest, I didn't have an answer
Some might think that if a poet isn't writing about their partner
That must mean that they are no longer in love
But I think for me, at least, it's the opposite
I used to write love poems in my singleness
Trying to create a fantasy where my love and I were finally in sync
And now I no longer have to dream
I wake up every morning next to a woman who I have loved a
thousand lifetimes
A woman who unravels my stage persona so I can simply be Brandon
I have no need for poetry when I'm with her
Because "I" becomes "we" when I'm with her
And that's the greatest poem God ever wrote
I write poems to heal from the wounds life has inflicted
I write poems to praise the moments in life that have brought me joy
I write poems to grow closer to God
And when I'm with you
I can do all three of those things without having to utter a word
Our love is music
Our marriage, the sweetest of melodies
Our time together, a beautiful harmony
Our future, the most intense of crescendos
And God, the tempo that ties it all together

# SPLINTERED

Girl, I don't know how you so splintered perfect
I don't mean to come off so wooden
But these burdens have rooted me in this melancholy
My only desire is to chop them up and carry them away
Whether by two-by-four
But . . .
It doesn't matter
I don't enjoy fantasies anymore
You know how many times I've been told to reach for the stars
To only wilt under the chill of their winter
To be snapped in half by the winds of their storm
To be burned to ash by the fire in their souls
Because if a soul splinters broken in the middle of a crowded forest
Will anyone care
Or will it just join the underbrush
To be the kindling for the next forest fire
To burn everything a cinder
To force someone else to start all over again

# TO MY SON

I'm looking forward to having children
And I pray to God
That my firstborn be a son
Knowing these genes
He'll be a spitting image of me
But I hope not
I do desire to see my reflection in him
Just not all of it
When he first comes to this world
I will treat him as an empty vessel
I shall force the best parts of me to sprout legs
Use these words as a map
So they can find their way to him
As for these formidable failings I bear
I shall press them to stained glass
Hang them up in the sanctuary of my temple
So when my son looks at his father
He can see all the things I've overcome
So the pitfalls that seduced me
Won't become a family legacy
That he may discover his masculinity isn't found in the suppression
of emotion
But in discernment on how to act on them
How his humanity isn't in how much weight he can bear
But instead in what he chooses to carry
How his value is not rooted in perfection
But how he can be flawed and loved at the same time
I want to have a son
Not so I can give him all the things I never had
But so I can teach him all the things it took me too long to learn
I want long car rides where I complain about how R&B ain't the
same no more
I want one-on-one games where I collect more fouls than points

I want conversations about his shortcomings and how he'll live and learn
I want to look into my son's eyes and learn
I want to learn the rhythm of how he desires to be loved
And be every bit of flawed human trying to be the tune he learns how
to two-step to
Until someone else sweeps him off his feet
And he remembers dad's old song about being weak in the knees
I want my son to grow older, and as I look at him
I want to see less of myself, more of God, and a whole lot of man
I'm proud to look at
I pray every night
That my firstborn be a son
Who is a better man than me

# MUTUALITY

God,
This world is crazy.
Witnessing all the things that go on,
I can understand
Why some folk don't believe in you.
Knowing you so powerful
But yet choose to let us be.
I understand that some can't see
How this love must be a choice
Or it becomes bondage in the worst sense.
But yo, God,
This place is crazy.
I live in a nation that prostituted your gospel
For the sake of their own empirical gain.
I live in a nation where folk who claim to serve you
Try to justify the murder of folk who look like me
Who then look at me and wonder why I question
What they see.
I live in a world that has substituted your naturally divine creation
For a concrete replica,
And we wonder why we feel so disconnected.
God, I love our freedom of choice,
It's just sometimes
I get tired of the decisions made for my sake.
Temperatures are rising, kingdoms are falling,
Humanity thinks of itself so highly these days;
The world is in disarray.
Which I know to you is nothing new.
Man . . .
I think I'm writing this poem; I'm starting to understand
That you
God
Are not distant, not far, not aloof,

But you're right by our side
Mourning too,
Just waiting, waiting for your creation
To choose to come back to you.

# ABIDE

Silence carries an eerie disposition
It either erodes away all semblance of tranquility
Or it engulfs one in amity's tenure
For so many years
The sheer hint of its presence
Left my poise awry
Contorted my typical opulence
Into a nexus of restless nervousness
To make it plain
Silence was an adversary all too grandiose
For me to face
Not due to stature
But in light of what it proposed
The ability to look in the mirror
And reflect on what was
I came to understand
My fear of silence was truly a fear of self
Of reconciling my generational echo
That reverberates across time
Until eternity comes to the scene to convene
All of who I am and once was
Already knowing all of who I will be
In attaining this wisdom
Silence sounds similar to serenity
Creating space to harmonize
With the God that exists inside of me
This Holy Spirit connection
Between a son and the Son
Is eroding all semblance of distress
Is engulfing me in amity's tenure
Abiding is a task one will never master
But must continually practice
Knowing that it is not a destination

But instead a journey
And if that isn't the most divine metaphor
For living in these fleshly beings
Then I don't know what is

# LONGBOARD

Your effortless glide across concrete
Is what draws me
When we are together
Bearing all the friction
That will occur
We have never been board
But forever flexible to the twists and turns
Along the road
While the eyes of the world
Breeze by
Their perception don't matter
They will only ever be able
To witness from the lens
Of a destination
And that don't matter either
All that amounts to anything
Is the current scene
Living in the midst of this moment's vitality
Knowing it may never feel like this again
The same way this breeze will never
Brush up against my face the same way twice
And there's something beautiful
About experiencing something for the first time
And last time
At the same time

# BE PRESENT

You know what, you can have tomorrow
And the next day, and the next day
I ain't worrying 'bout it no more
For too long has my anticipation of tomorrow
Ruined my joy of the present

# TRAILS

I wonder, do trails get lost
I wonder, do trails get lost when people abandon them
To start their own path
Or is it like giving birth
A beautifully painful experience
Accompanied by long hours
The yielding result being
More precious than they ever imagined
I wonder, do trails remember their birthing
When the world was young
And humanity had yet prostitute their mother's nature
I wonder, do trails hate how humanity treads on them
Or is it something they've grown accustomed to
I wonder, do trails think back in time
Before they became paved
Desiring to be undone
To be overgrown again
To be wild and untamed again
I wonder, do trails consider
That's why humanity made them
So they can feel undone
Feel wild and untamed again
Never caring about who they cauterized to do so
I wonder, do trails ever burn with hate
For humanity's apathy
I wonder, do trails get lost in thought
About all they've lost
I wonder . . .

# JOYOUS POET'S DEATH

(Golf clap)
That was aite
But
Where the blood at
I thought you knew
No matter what time
You stepped on this stage
You became a sacrifice
So you betta bleed for me
You know this culture is so enamored by agony
And no one escapes assimilation's initiation
That's why joy don't comfort me
I only find peace in painful poems
For all my aches are numb
Under the weight of someone else's pain
That's why when I revel in yours
Be sure to stitch them wounds up
With the loose threads of these scores
For agony don't console the soul
When it's too close in proximity
But when you're on stage
Mirror, my malady
Cause misery loves company
Remember
You supposed to bleed for me, not on me
Bloodstains don't come out easy
And can't you see
I'm already bleeding

# LOADED BASES

The time is coming;
We need to get into formation.
The block is hot,
And my folk known for catching cases.
But ain't no time for that,
I tell them they need a li'l patience.
I'm praying to God that they embrace it
With these loaded bases.

In life, I'm just trying to
Maneuver around these land mines
To try and land mine.
Cause too much pressure
At the right spot but the wrong time,
Could lead this black man
Six feet deep with flat vital signs.
While me and Nightingale
Just trying to avoid hell or jail cells,
And we won't fail.
I've poured all my life into plan A,
Intently illustrating this immaculate image
Of how we turned this rocky soil we're given
Into a ravishing forest to feed the village we live in.
No more surviving, we living.
With this excess now, we giving
No more need for set tripping,
Just sit back, relax, and peep the vision.
Particularly placing people in they set position.
It take a li'l time and effort,
But this endeavor gone complete the mission.
This is the final phase of how we end division (the vision).
The troops are now in the right places.
I'm staring at loaded bases,
Knowing damn well I'm gon' Willie Mays it.

The time is coming;
We need to get into formation.
The block is hot,
And my folk known for catching cases.
But ain't no time for that,
I tell them they need a li'l patience.
I'm praying to God that they embrace it
With these loaded bases.

# REIGN

It rained yesterday
Raindrops like bullets
Fell from the sky
And after the storm
I heard a slew of birds singing
It sounded like
They were letting each other know
That they made it through the rain alive
Kinda like a celebration
And a mourning song for those they lost
And for me
It was . . .
Breathtaking

It rained today
Bullets like raindrops
Shot through the air
And after the storm
I saw all my neighbors come out
Wide-eyed and lips shut
It looked like
They were letting each other know
That they made it through the rain alive
Kinda like a celebration
And a moment of silence
For those we lost
And unfortunately for some
It was breathtaking

# ANVILS

What a beautiful sight it is
Seeing souls set free
Through a barrage of words
Fluttering about a room
Like anvils do when they meet gravity
Plummeting to the ground
The way it hit felt like freedom
Because merely existing is
Seeing tongues shackled
By populous recollections
Of inadequacies
But that definition ain't adequate
Existing feels like molting an exoskeleton
And you're not strong enough
To break out of it
But my voice is
When finally utilized to dismantle these lies
But I mask my insecurities with humility
Tell the rest of the world to shine bright
Inform them that
I'll be the pedestal they do it on
Ignoring the fact that I've never been nightstand
But daybreak
I am the sunrise of a dawn
I've always feared
Knowing twilight will inevitably
Meet me on the other side
I'm realizing what's really shackled my voice
Has been my own hesitancy to be free
Fearing that my ascension will be met with dissension
For so long, I've lived on y'all acceptance
And been dying by y'all rejection
But no matter how much you chase the night

You can't evade sunrise
Destiny will come for you and that gift you've shelved
Knowing damn well it don't expire
I come to open mics
To witness caterpillars liberate themselves
From an entrapment of their own design
Just hoping that one day
That could be me

# LUSTING OVER LOSS

Once
I tried to synthesize love into
A refined liquid
No drug addict
But still, typical trope
Eloped with this dope
In search of hope
Figured I'd take a smack at it
So why not
Needles up, shooting up
Just for it to dissipate in vein
I hoped it would be the solution
To this affliction
Of how my heart hasn't knocked
On my chest cavity door
Since I've grown hollow
I long to be immersed
Because I've found love to be vast
But shallow
The irony that I want someone
To love and hold me
When I won't give them
The whole me
Out of fear they'll find the holes in me
My friends told me to try intimacy
A fast-track wave of emotional bliss
With none of the scary commitment
Not understanding I'm not afraid of love's longevity
I'm afraid of its climax
That I'll be head over heels in what I perceive to be love
To find out I've simply been someone's erotic fantasy
That they never wanted me to hold them
Or embrace the whole them

They didn't even want me to see the holes in them
They just wanted me to fit in the hole in them
Being a black man in a sexually racist world
I've encountered numerous girls who have wanted nothing more from me
Than what they hope to be is a lengthy extremity
I guess I'm better at understanding what it's like to be a woman
Seeing that someone saw me as an elementary school puzzle
Fit the round peg in the square hole
When I just wanted to be the missing piece
In each other's incomplete jigsaw
What hurts most is
I gave in

# GRAVE MISTAKES

My greatest adversary is time
This never-ending battle of trying to hold on to youth
But with age comes wisdom
And I've learned that growing old is a blessing
Cause I know folks in the yard
Who made grave mistakes
And they taught me that aging is a privilege
That they weren't privy to

# SOUF

I ain't nothing but a south side Stockton kid
And I still remember them days
When the block be hot as spring end
Cause all these hood boys
Trying to lose weight and catch a summer body
Though they never picked up a book
They was all on the same page
My whole neighborhood was chasing a bag
It's sad cause that's how most of them ended up in one
Example
Gunshots rang through the streets
A young boy walked out
Saw his father's DNA spread round the block
At that moment, he knew his pops was never coming home
Momma always told him his dad was a rolling stone
This the place where folks willingly exchange
Button ups for zippers
Turned the hood into Eden the way they found dough in the garden
Rediscovered fire, then got it sparking
And you wonder how we praise God in the middle of all this
Well . . .
The distance between Heaven and Earth is six feet
And we already inching into the grave
No wonder why all my folk trying to get saved

# ADVENT

The Old Testament speaks of the day Jesus would come
For in the blankness of the void
Before existence was a word
Resting on the lips of creation
Laid the one and only hope of the world
For "In the beginning was the Word, and the Word was with God,
and the Word was God"
It speaks of a time in which nations would crumble
When the skies would roar and turn ablaze at
His sight
When the Earth herself would tremble knowing . . .
That in humanity's darkest hour
GOD in flesh . . .
The undeserved hope of the world . . .
Traversed the path from Heaven to Earth
To grace her again
For the sake of healing the ailment of sin
This is the story of Jesus
A Prince of Peace who gave every single piece
Of himself for the sake of his bride
But before that could ever occur he graced Earth in the most
Humbling of ways
Because the skies did not crackle
Nor did they split to the outpour of Heaven's fury
Instead, it was a night where a cloudy haze with but one star in the
sky shone
Guiding a few souls to deliver devotion to the newborn king
The Earth did not rumble
Nor succumb to rubble
Instead, she remained silent, eerily still
As the streets of Bethlehem riddled with the desolation
A cool winter's eve brings in its wake
While a woman carrying the light of the world was denied asylum

By the very people who prayed for the gift she carried
But that's how the Son of man came to Earth
Not only in the humility of flesh
But in the humility of a manger
When the whole world should have fallen to its knees
In praise of his arrival
But instead, he was forced to be a refugee
Fleeing from a fear mongering ruler
Who would have thought that a little brown-skinned boy
Being birthed in a trough where swine came to dine
Would be humanity's greatest gift
And it is this, this most certain act of selfless love
That is the reason for the season
Yet so many of us get enamored by the craze
Taking advantage of this day
To seek self-centered validation through the means
Of financial promiscuity
Looking to bolster our self-worth
From the adoration of others
While allowing for those on the margins
The ones who have nothing to account for
Besides what they carry on they backs
To perpetually live in lack
This is the season where we display our humanity
Allow us to no longer be ignorant of ways of Christ
We humble ourselves to the grandeur God
Knowing that the return of the Messiah is soon coming
And this time, we wait in undying anticipation
With hearts prepared to give all unto you
And hands ready to receive all of you in return
That this time, our streets not be riddled by the desolation
Of a cold, apathetic heart, but instead, we allow our homes
And these bodies to be a safe haven

For that's what Christ did for us
Took our sins, housed them in a residence of flesh
Took them to the grave
And left them there to stay
Our God, who art in Heaven Hallowed be thy name
Thy Kingdom come Thy will be done
On Earth as it is in Heaven
And let this day
Not fade away without our remembrance
That a child was born

# FLINT

Flint, Michigan still ain't got clean water.
If I didn't utter another word,
That would still be enough of a poem.
Because Flint, Michigan still ain't got clean water.
And no one cares.
No one cares that these lead pipes
Have led lead through the inner workings of these bodies
Like sewage systems
But these aren't corroding pipelines,
These are eroding lifelines.
But what's new?
Flint, Michigan is fifty-seven percent black,
And we know America has always considered us
A pollutant to their distilled existence,
So this ain't nothing more than another way
For them to try and filter us out.
But understand . . .
Black folks have been the charcoal in your system
That has filtered your racism into profit
Since its inception,
But be warned: charcoal that has been overused
Can most certainly
Kill you.

# OUR MISTRESS

Death is the mistress
We were all arranged to marry
Knowing nothing about
The life to come after her embrace
But we knew that her touch would change us
So we try to hold on to sanity
Get a grip on our perceived reality
Only to realize that everything comes undone
Holding on to life is like hugging a jigsaw puzzle
Feeling it crumble in your arms
Just hoping the pieces fall into place
It can be difficult to find joy
In the temporary
To know it will inevitably come to an end
That makes life more strenuous
Straining to remain vigilant
Ever focused on survival
Because the moment you slip
Is the moment you begin to exchange those eternal vows
And joy is a slippery slope, but stoicism ain't
It makes the fall numb
It dulls the senses under the illusion of control
When in actuality
All it ever did was rob us of this gift
Called the present

# KOBE

I know it may be weird to write a goodbye letter
To a man you've never met
But I don't care
Kobe
You were more than a basketball player to me
You
You were the idol of my drive
You looked at how talent never failed to meet hard work in your presence
You overachieved in the face of opposition without a word of complaint
Took that mamba mentality from my time on the court
To my time with a pad
And seeing you transition from hooper to dad
That's what broke me when you left
Imagining the seconds passing by that must have felt like eternity
Holding your daughter in your arms knowing there was nothing you
could do
And I know you
You study film to the T
Know how to respond to everything the defense gives you
So I'm sure your instincts kicked in
When things weren't going according to plan
You assessed the situation
Looked out the window
Because it's never about the first defender
The helicopter is the first defender
And it won't kill you
But the ground will
And the ground is the second defender
The one you stare at
Then try to look off
In hopes to manipulate how it will respond to your move
But the third defender is the most treacherous
It's the one that dictates your next move

And I know that's where you froze for the first time
The third defender was your daughter
And at this point, everything stopped
Fear and instinct melted away knowing that the last thing y'all will
share is this moment
And I couldn't imagine
I couldn't imagine the prayers you sent up
How you knew God was more clutch than you
And how every prayer is answered
Just not always the way we expect
I wonder, did you ever look at that second defender again
Or did you just stop with the third
Because it didn't matter no more
The game wasn't being played at this time
It was just a daughter and her dad
Exchanging "I love you's" that will never fade away
Kobe, you taught me to never lose touch with the moment
To value every opportunity you have as if it were your last
To leave all of yourself on the court
On the page
Or whatever battlefield you took war on
And in the loss of you and your daughter, I realize
You never took your eyes or arms off her
Because she was the most valuable prize you'd ever hold on to
I wonder how you felt knowing the clock was running out
But knowing the game wasn't in your hands
And still with your daughter in your arms
Your greatest victory was already in your grasp
And you didn't want it to be

# MOMENT

I'll never have this moment again
It will never be
11:47 p.m. on January 31, 2020, again
It will never be you and I
Here laid up in this bed together
The same way we are right now
Again
And there's something Beautiful about it
And there's something Frightening about it
Let's go bad news first
It's scary to think
As this ink slinks from pen to pad
That I'll never be this man again
So joyous
So caught in the moment
That writing this poem was difficult
Because for a moment, you and I existed outside of time
When everything froze
When nothing else mattered
And there's beauty in stillness
And fear is not knowing
If it will ever come back
But in this moment
I refuse to any longer lease my joy
To relinquish it back to my fear
I have paid in full my dues
Blood, sweat, and tears
Sleepless nights pondering life's existentialism
No, no more
For we'll never be here again
Never be this Brandon again
And I want to remember him as joyous
Want my recollections

Of a man that time carried to a new day
To not be riddled with worry about tomorrow
Because tomorrow will take care of itself

# BLACK BOY JOY

Be forewarned
This poem is dangerous
This poem is unapologetically black
But this ain't your typical black poem
This poem is not the absence of light
But the source in which it radiates from
This poem is black excellence
This here is black boy joy
Have you ever seen a black boy fly
I have . . .
I remember the first time I looked in the mirror
After getting them J's
Felt like Lonnie Carmon
Soaring through the skies of Ohio
My soul never even touched the ground
I got heroine in my smile
Cocaine in my laughter
These words that hit the block harder
Than the crack epidemic
Verses laced with substance more potent
Than something forced
To fentanyl psyches of black men
And can mend the hearts of open chests
Just as well as Dr. Williams ever did
Now don't let my black boy joy fool you
I still reside in a culture
That would much rather
Wear my skin to appropriate its likeness
Than to allow it to live freely on its own
It's easier to marionette the flesh
Than to try and cohere the soul
But mind you that is not the purpose of this poem
We are more than our pain

More than the fact that
Our ancestors were not slaves
They were prisoners of a war
They wanted no part of
And I will be the symbol of their liberation
No longer leasing my joy to these
Momentary highs
Naw, I'm addicted to the real thing
And self-love is addictive
And dangerous
When you live in a country
That's always wanted you
But never said dead or alive
But that's not the point of this poem
This is about generational restoration
Like Dr. Sebi said
We healing these holes with holistic healing
And the best form of medication
Is a smile
And joy is infectious, so spread it round
It is our greatest form of resistance
To live a life that is our own
That's the root of this poem
Recognizing that when you walk
Through the streets of any city
You will see our fingerprints
And how we lay claim
To black excellence

# IDIOCY

Imagine . . .
Willingly subjecting yourself to a task
That wears down your soul
More quickly than a momma's patience
With two kids in a grocery store
Who have hands of adhesive
And arms of elastic
This is what it feels like to walk into work most mornings
To stare at a building and contemplate
All the ways you can make that thang burn
Without it looking like arson
I mean, Sheryl always has her space heater
A bit too close to the trash can at her desk
So a loose paper or two here
Mixed with a "crank up to high heat" there
And (fire sound)
I got at least a few days off before they elect
To have us continue working in the remains
But ain't that capitalism
See, you burn to death in an attempt to court her
But once you've smoldered to ash
She'll still say you ain't urned a burial
But I'll still be here at work tomorrow
Trying to fit my God-sized dreams
Into this nine by five cubicle
While simultaneously trying to two-step to the tune of my aspiration
And my coworkers is irritated
They say I'm far too loud
And absorbing too much real estate
Well, Sheryl, I'm so sorry my aspirations require
More space than your heater
But maybe one day you'll realize the only reason this office is so cold
Is because it's become a morgue

To store the dreams you let die
Or maybe this has always been you
Maybe this space hasn't caused your soul to atrophy
Maybe I am taking up too much space in your home
But understand I have no choice
Capitalism has forced my residency in currency
Which I've never found value in
But it's the only thing this country be valuing
As for me
I'd rather find value and purpose
Through the continuance of new experiences
Discovering home in every place
I press pen to pad on
Allow for the world to be my stage
And the curtain only closes
For my after-party in Heaven
There's something divine about that
Writing these poems
Is the closest I've ever felt to God
The way I can turn ink into a universe
With the sway of my hand
No wonder why God chose words
To bring light to existence
It's the most powerful thing you can ever share
They say if you love what you do
Then you'll never work a day in your life
Well, I want to spend mine
Creating stories as frequently
As I create memories
In doing that, I know
That all the sweat, tears, and blood I shed
Will not have been in vain
But that's just me

Maybe you, Cheryl
Have found vitality within these four walls
Maybe you've discovered home in a routine
That you can lean on
Found your love in the consistency this place brings
I'm not trying to knock yo' nine-to-five hustle
But the parts of myself I love most
Are dying here
Under this frigid regime
Creativity curbed, free reins downpour ceased
They threw a book at me
Said I live or die by the code
And my soul caught hypothermia
America loves art
They love they movies, music, and museums
But it hates the artists that breathe life into them
They demand our art
But they deny us our living
They say artists make their best art
When they feel they are closest to the grave
No wonder they try to starve us

# FATIGUE

These days, I wear a worn-out soul
Like distressed fatigues
I'm a soldier
It's my job to fight
Or so they say
See, I wasn't born with options
No
The choice to fight on this battlefield of equality
Is a luxury only afforded to my opposition
They live in a world of . . .
"Normalcy"
They don't understand the pains
Scrubbing layers of yourself off
Without an ounce of paint thinner
They know nothing of this
They exist in
Ignorant bliss that if they so choose
They can completely ignore the gunshots
Hiding behind a wall of privilege
But don't tell them this
The idea of their safety
Not being commonality
Infuriates them
Makes them feel like less of an underdog
And you know how America loves its bootstraps
As for me
Well, round here we've rounded up
Rounds of ammunition shells
Smelted those into armor
Because bullets are rolling stones
Once they've left the barrel
They never return
Only finding home in the flesh of strange fruit

And maybe if we camouflage ourselves in its likeness
It won't want to welcome itself here
But that's only wishful thinking
Wise tales and myths passed on from former generations
But there is wisdom in their stories
The way they understood the very thing
That killed them and passed on the knowledge before the eulogy
Hid divine truths in odd places
Like spirituals
Knowing our oppressor would get lost in the rhythm
But we could decipher the code
Unfortunately, many of my folk don't listen to the past too much
Prefer to blaze their own trail
Unfortunately, there's nothing new under the sun
They walk trampled paths made by those
Daring enough to say "enough"
I wonder how it felt
For those who first felt the uneasiness of virgin sand
Sifting between their toes
Did they feel liberated, or did it feel like quicksand

# SMA

My mind is weary
And my heart is broken
But my soul is rich
And my spirit never fading
This flesh I'm in is weak
Longs for justice's bastard cousin
Revenge
Longs for my oppressor to feel
The pain he has caused me
But my spirit knows the war will not be won this way
Knows that I may win a battle
Swing my fists like my great-great-grandfather
Swung noosed hung from trees
Throw hands like they threw bombs
At my great-grandmother in the churches of Selma
Thrust my knees through chest cavities
Like bullets through Philando, Trayvon, Terence
My flesh longs for retribution of their crimes against me
There will be no justice until there is justice for me
But my spirit knows lasting progress doesn't reside here
Doesn't reside within the crimson walls of revenge
But my soul isn't silent
It isn't quiet, it isn't in compliance
It screams and shouts for the ones who have been taken
Because we didn't lose them
For being lost is an accident
They were taken by choice
And my soul's voice beacons me into action
Calls me to disturb their comfortability
So yes, I stand in the midst of freeway entrances
Because this nation can no longer try and move forward
While leaving us behind
I raise my voice in the streets, on stages, at churches, in the workplace

Because an injustice anywhere is a threat to justice everywhere
I take knees as the song of this nation rings through stadiums
For I am Shadrach
I am Meshach
I am Abednego refusing to bow at the altar
Of the false God
America has become
And has always been
With every bit of conviction in my soul, I vow
To represent my Lord and Savior on the front lines of oppression vs.
justice
With loving accountability
I fight only for the things I care about
So America, understand I care about you
I care about you enough that
I vow to raise my voice as an act of violent protest
For every word I speak is an attack on our society
That oppresses black people so normally
I vow to make this nation better today than it was yesterday
By dragging it toward the ideals it preaches
I vow to be the church in action
For peace and God are one and the same
I dare us all to remember *imago Dei*
And how the only way All Lives Matter
Is if Black Lives Matter

# THE NEXT MOURNING

Have you ever watched a building burn
It's strange
The way it sets ablaze
Cause no matter where the fire started
The inside always burns up first
It's crazy the similarity
The way a riot in my chest left me lifeless
Vacant
Burned from the inside out
But the funniest part is
Everyone is so concerned about the building
They act as if
I'm not the one smoldering

# BREONNA

First and foremost
I will not apologize for this piece
The utilization of my voice
To speak for those whose absence
From this Earth beckons my pen
To scribble them back into existence
And since God gave me this gift
I must use it for His people
Breonna Taylor
You will forever live within the ink of this pen
And on the forefront of my conscious
You were an EMT in the process of becoming a nurse
You carried love in excess
Cared for others you possessed
A beloved daughter you were
A diamond on full display
The way you rocked for your community
So clear to see
4K plus ten
You were a shining example of hope to your family and friends
And it hurts me that I got to speak of your name in the past tense
Or that I have to list your accomplishments
Just for people's consciousness to perceive or receive
Your humanity as valuable
The way our culture will dig up a person's past
Before we've even dug a grave
Just so they can justify they hate
So let's address these elephants in the room
No, Breonna wasn't fired as an EMT
She was still joyfully employed
No, Breonna wasn't responsible for a body in that trunk
That man was apprehended and pled guilty to the crime
No, Breonna wasn't smuggling drugs, nor was her boyfriend at the time

AND NO, BREONNA DIDN'T DESERVE TO DIE
EVEN IF ALL THAT PRECEDED THIS WERE TRUE
She should have been given her due process
But instead, bullets in excess
Came through and repossessed
A beloved daughter
A diamond on full display
So clear to see
And I know what some of y'all thinking
And I agree
All cops ain't bad
The same way all blacks ain't criminals
But question: how am I to tell the difference
Between a good cop versus a bad cop
When they both function in a broken system
And the good cop is complicit
Breonna, the tragic result of your hearing
Came on one of the biggest days of my life
I know this poem ain't much
But I hope the movement of my pen
Can help make it right

# RUNNING OUT

I feel like I'm running out of time
Ever since I won *AGT*
I feel like the clock been ticking
And it's as if
I ain't got but so long
Until the rug gets pulled from up underneath me
And I'm back to my former normality
Now there's nothing wrong with the past
But I've grown to know
That it belongs behind me
Instead of it becoming my destiny
And I guess that's what I'm afraid of
I'm afraid of having come so far
To only have come but so far
Having battled for so long for the sake of this dream
I thought winning would be liberating
But instead, I feel like I'm skating on thin ice
Above the bitter cold reality of what happens
When opportunity stares you in the face
And elects to pass you by
And I'm terrified
I'm terrified of the falling
That's why I was always afraid to journey this high
Carrying all this weight
And nowadays, I can't tell if I'm bearing this burden
Due to my strength or numbness
But either way, I'm tired
Mind racing about everything standing in my way
Ignoring the fact that I just did something only fourteen others in
the world had done
It's hard to find happiness
When anxiety has found a home in the cracks of your victories
Laid clear a path for insecurity

But if there is one thing I've learned, it's that happiness is fleeting
And joy is a choice
I can't speak for tomorrow
But in this moment
I will choose mountaintop joy
Even though
I'm horrified of heights

# FRIENDS

If I'm being honest
I don't really have friends
At least not now anyway
I feel like a mirage
Like people can see me
Just not for what's actually there
And I don't know who's to blame
If it's me or them
Because I come up here on this stage
And I show the world who I am
Bare and unbridled
And yet somehow, I'm still lost to the crowd
Maybe they struggle finding me
Amidst the fog of metaphors and double entendres
So hi
My name is Brandon
I'm a black kid from south side Stockton
I'm in love with Jesus
And even though I believe in Yahweh
I still fear the grave
And all of its unknowing
I love anime
Like *Yu Yu Hakusho* is so underrated
G Gundam is the best Gundam ever made
And yes, Goku could beat Superman
I'm a basketball head
I still do the Euro step every time
I step around something in my house
And I critique refs as if I'd like to have their job
I love deeply
And I think that scares people
I know it scares me
Because sometimes I get so lost in trying to love others

I forget how to receive love for myself
And when I finally find my way
I feel guilty for actually asking for it
I love writing poetry
It's one of the few times I actually feel seen
Everyone thinks I'm this social butterfly
Not understanding I've always been a magician
Using the art of misdirection to fool audiences
Into believing my magic
When I'm truly just cocooned in the background
I write poems about healing and reconciliation
Because I hope that this last one will be the last one
But life's a journey and not a destination
So I don't know who I'm fooling
I'm just a scared man
Lost at sea
I'm . . .
Lost you see
Trying to anchor down on something real
Something tangible enough for me to hook my love on to
No more mirages
No more metaphors
Just honesty
So honestly, can you be my friend
I could really use one

# FAKE FRIENDS

You think you got fake friends, please
My friends so fake
That I don't even get birthday texts no more
My friends so fake
My birthday passes by more frequently than they do
My friends so fake
I can count on one hand how many times
I've seen them in the last year
My friends so fake
I put they faces on milk cartons
So it don't hurt so much when they ain't there
My friends so fake
They complain about why we ain't talked in so long
Not realizing a phone work both ways
My friends so fake
It's like they were never there in the first place
But their impact was so real
Like a mirage in the heat of this barren dessert
Even though you know in the bottom of your soul
That it's not there
The disappointment of its evaporation still leaves you thirsty for
something real
My friends so fake
That they don't know I've been suffering internally to the point
That I haven't seen the outside of my room in days
My friends so fake
They fell for the mirage of social media
They see me post and think they know how I've been
But if they would just come close enough, they'd realize
It was all a facade
They'd see a dehydrated soul just longing to be quenched

# SIMPLE

You ever just sit on your porch and contemplate
Listen to how everything around you is moving
How life is really happening
These existential moments make you realize how small you are
And how much more there is to this world besides you
But with the time given, what will you do
Yahweh had a specific purpose in mind when he designed you
A seed knows not what it shall become once it is planted
All it knows is circumstances in which it exists
And that in order to survive, it must never remain static
It must do what it was created to do
And grow

# DAWGS

If all my Dawgs go
To Heaven, is that where my
School reunion is?

# ANOTHER ONE

The masses said Brandon
Another black man died
Can you give us another poem Brandon
You are the voice of the people
Please give us another poem (breathe)
How loud do you have to knock
On a coffin's door
Before the dead will rise
For a black man, there is no knock
Even after death, we are asked to entertain you
Motivate you
Be a backbone, so this world won't break you
You ever seen a parade of dead black men
March down the street
I promise you have
Just attend any protest
You'll see the scattered pieces of their bodies
Spread so thin amongst the rage
You'll only ever hear his name

# FATHER'S LOVE

How to describe a father's love
Imagine a caged lion
But this cage ain't stagnant
It operates in a ten-foot radius
Of every place she goes
So try her
And in turn, try me
And realize just how omnipresent I can be
And when these fists
Elect to remove teeth on a five-finger discount
I'll still expect change on your account
But ain't it funny how my kiss and my fist
Are both a sign of care
What I'm saying is
My love is immutable
It just feels different pending on the recipient
What's most crazy to me
Is how much I see God in both these actions
How He'll care enough to place a blessing on my cheek
And in the same motion, put a boot on the throat of my enemy

# ETERNAL CONFLICT

I've lived my life conflicted
Either overly concerned about not doing enough for the kingdom
Or too laxed to be bothered to move
Transitioned from Deficiencies declaring dominion over my life
To my petulant pride propagating through my being
This is the life of a man bound by the pendulum
Forever destined to swing between extremes
To only momentarily experience the grace of just being
Aligned with the peace that surpasses understanding
And I've felt this my whole life
Spent my childhood days learning to count as the seconds went by
Without ever learning how to count on God
Cause I'm too knuckleheaded for that
Can't seem to wrap my fingers around the fact
That these hands can't do any more work
Than pierced palms already have
And that's okay
But it shouldn't breed complacency
And I just can't seem to find a healthy understanding
Of where God's responsibility ends and where mine begins
But maybe that's not how it goes
Maybe instead of racing against the clock
I should just submit my time
To the one who exists outside of it
But there's this dead space between time and eternity
Where it feels like everything erodes away
No such thing as time, and nothing matter
Can withstand the disappearing act that this place will make you endure
But there is something beautiful about being undone
Where the only thing left standing is your soul
And there's no more labor to be had
No more tugging and pulling
Just existing, finally understanding how

Human is being both flawed and unblemished
Constantly being made whole while being perfect at the same time
No more reckless ball swinging from one destructive extreme to the next
I'm slowing down
So I can get this vertical right
Cause that's the only way this pendulum will ever get centered
I guess what I'm saying is
My whole life, I've felt at unease
Like resting ain't bring peace
Cause I was sprinting against the clock
But I'm learning that the best way
To win this race against time
Is to not let it run by
And maybe that's where my responsibility begins
In recognizing that time is a blessing instead of an adversary

# ELEVATION

I hate flying
The coast part is beautiful
But the part of the flight
Where the nose turns up
And everything floats for a brief moment
I can't stand it
The constant ascension to new heights
Admittedly, it scares the hell out of me
Although the view is heavenly
The only thing that I can think about
Is the comedown
And not the gradual descent
No, the cataclysmic crash-landing
Where no one survives
I can't get it out of my head
I pray for the release of these fears
But
As the vessel continues to climb
My anxieties rise
So I guess I sincerely am not afraid of the height
But instead of falling out of the sky
And I think that's the biggest metaphor of my career fear

# INDEX

Enjoy *Unraveling* as an audiobook narrated by the author, wherever audiobooks are sold.

Andrews McMeel Publishing
a division of Andrews McMeel Universal
1130 Walnut Street, Kansas City, Missouri 64106

www.andrewsmcmeel.com

22 23 24 25 26 VEP 10 9 8 7 6 5 4 3 2 1

ISBN: 978-1-5248-7055-3

Library of Congress Control Number: 2021946053

Editor: Patty Rice
Art Director/Designer: Spencer Williams
Production Editor: Jasmine Lim
Production Manager: Carol Coe

ATTENTION: SCHOOLS AND BUSINESSES
Andrews McMeel books are available at quantity discounts with bulk purchase for educational, business, or sales promotional use. For information, please e-mail the Andrews McMeel Publishing Special Sales Department:
specialsales@amuniversal.com.